INTRODUCTION

The deserts of the world have a spirit all their own. These desolate, empty landscapes reach deep into the soul, eliciting a profound response. They are full of romance and danger. To think of the North African Sahara is to conjure images of slow Bedouin caravanserai winding their way over the dunes that rise and fall like waves on an endless sea of sand. To journey in the imagination to the vast outback of Australia is to take part in the Aboriginal dreamtime during which the primordial ancestors dreamed the world into existence, laying every sacred contour of each hill and valley. To step outside the bustle of the urban world into the American deserts is to be immersed in the mystery of solitude, which bares down on the soul like the burning sun.

The desert landscapes of the Middle East have inspired three of the great world religions — Judaism, Christianity, and Islam — as well as the ancient Egyptian religion, which illuminated the ancient Pagan world for more than five thousand years. Moses led his people across these deserts in search of the promised land. The early Christian "Desert Fathers" inhabited the tombs of dead pharaohs, desert caves, and solitary cells, where they lived as hermits

communing with God. Muhammad loved the deserts and mountains where he would go to meditate on Allah. It was here that he received visions of the angel Gabriel who dictated to him the Holy Koran, the sacred scripture of Islam. Islamic mystics, called Sufis, told stories about the desert to teach the faithful. Collectively they present a rich testament to the power of the desert to awaken the spiritual fire of the human imagination.

DESERT FEELINGS

THE DESERT has many faces and evokes many feelings. It is a place whose awesome expanses speak of beauty, freedom, and death. To escape the power of the sun under the shadow of the pyramids or the sphinx is to be drawn back into the ancient world, when Ra the sun-god was worshiped morning and evening as he sailed his sky-boat across the heavens to delineate the day and night. To sky-watch on a desert night is to be over-awed by the population of shining stars, more numerous than the human beings that throng the cities, a still and silent contrast to our cacophony of business. For the Sufi poet Rumi a journey into the desert was a metaphor for the soul setting off into the Void of God. The caravanserai is ready to depart and the heavenly drum is sounding "let's go!"

*L*overs, listen!

The time to leave this world has come.

My inner ear can hear

the heavenly drum sounding "let's go!".

Look! The camel driver is awake.

The camels are ready.

If you are a traveler,

why are you still sleeping?

Everywhere is the din of departure.

Each moment a soul is setting off into the Void.

You've fallen into a deep sleep;

as heavy as this life is light.

Soul, look for the Soul!

Friend, look for the Friend!

Watchmen should watch out, not doze off!

The streets are full of candles and torches,

clamor and confusion,

for tonight this changing world

gives birth to something eternal.

You were desert dust, but are now the wind.

You were foolish but are now made wise.

JALALUDIN RUMI

HYMN IN PRAISE OF

RA THE SUN-GOD

Blessings to You,

fierce fiery hawk,

as dreadful and beautiful as love.

Your light has burst upon the land,

like yellow pollen on a bee's back.

The gods are all singing,

intoxicated with your light.

It is Ra who gathers the world together,

springing from the formless water,

and taking the form of fire.

Like the first word,

he is uttered from the horizon's mouth.

Like music he passes through the heavens.

As long as the sun sings,

the strings of my lyre-like heart

vibrate a hymn in unison with him.

Until evening, may I walk under the sun,

forgetting time and reason.

May I explode with light,

like a purple flower of remembrance.

The air cracks and the sun beats its rhythm.

Everyday – the sun.

Everyday.

ANCIENT EGYPTIAN HYMN

O God, thou art my God; early will I seek thee;

my soul thirsteth for thee, my flesh longeth for thee

in a dry and thirsty land, where no water is;

To see thy power and thy glory,

so as I have seen these in the sanctuary.

Because thy loving kindness is better than life,

my lips shall praise thee.

Thus will I bless thee while I live:

I will lift up my hands in thy name.

My soul shall be satisfied as with marrow and fatness;

and my mouth shall praise thee with joyful lips:

When I remember thee upon my bed,

and meditate on thee in the night watches.

Because thou hast been my help,

therefore in the shadow of thy wings I rejoice.

PSALM 63

Lawrence of Arabia found much in common with his servant Dahoum. Lawrence was always deeply grateful to him for opening his mind to the solitude of the desert.

He recalls in The Seven Pillars of Wisdom "At last Dahoum drew me: 'Come and smell the very sweetest scent of all,' and we went to the main lodging, to the gaping window sockets of its eastern face, and there drank with open mouths of the effortless, empty, eddyless wind of the desert, throbbing past."

T.E. LAWRENCE

The sun was so hot I was cooking. It was a lonely and exhilarating feeling to see no signs of human hands. No houses, cars, supermarkets, telephone booths. No quick fix in an emergency. Just the cacti rising up against the blue horizon. Some of them twice the size of a man. Some reaching straight up like giant phalluses. Others with two outstretched arms like a human figure. These were my only companions – the men of the desert. I wandered over to one of these burly natives who seemed as permanently angry as the blazing sun. I sat in what little shade there was to drink some water. It was so cool on my throat. I splashed my face – and then it happened. It was as if the great empty sky, my angry cactus friend, and the parched ground beneath me were all shaking with one tremendous pulse of power and a voice, like the voice of the desert, spoke in my ear saying "You are alive!"

STEPHEN ARMSTRONG

Oh that the desert were my dwelling place,

With only one fair spirit for my minister.

That I might all forget the human race,

And hating no one, love her only.

GEORGE GORDON, LORD BYRON

A man can only be free in the desert.

ARAB PROVERB

In the desert
  of the heart,
Let the healing
  fountain start;
In the prison
  of his days,
Teach the free man
  how to praise.

W.H. AUDEN

Go walkabout in the outback then you feel it. You feel it there. We say "djang" – mean energy, power – somethin'. It strong there. You go see like Katatjula – Uluru – other place – sacred place – nice place. You look, but not go there. These day they crawling on Uluru (Ayers Rock) like ants, they don't know why. I don't know why. These places put there in "Tjukurrpa" – Dreamtime – by the Old Ones. Go there with good heart and you feel djang – much power, energy. I'm tellin' you.

BILL BUNGABE

The Nazca Desert is a barren expanse. Flat open nothingness with a shallow overlay of small stones. But the winds are few there and if you kick some of these small stones, where you have walked you will leave your mark for a thousand years. Some years ago someone flew over this desert in a little plane and saw the lines. Long straight lines reaching to the horizon, carefully constructed and clearly delineated. And then the animals – pictures in the desert created by the simple removal of the stones – a monkey, a condor, a spider. The sacred animals of our ancestors, waiting to be seen by someone who flies high enough. Great emblems marked into the very landscape for some magical purpose. Look from the ground and you see nothing. Look from the air and you see everything. I often wonder what our ancestors meant to say to us by this. They had no airplanes. Did these shamans fly up into the sky? What are these mysterious forms? I don't know, but whenever I walk the great spider or dance the lines of the monkey, I feel the blood of my ancient forbears still coursing in my veins and a strange delight fills me.

MARCUS APPOLATIO

There is no sight like the desert night. So many stars I have never seen before. I wandered off from the fire and settled myself onto the back of a dune like a sofa.

I lay down and looked up. There above me was Orion, one of the few constellations that I easily recognize. The ancient Egyptians knew this pattern of stars as the god Osiris – Lord of the Dead. And at his feet is Sirius, the dog star, which they associated with the goddess Isis. The Egyptians believed that each soul is also a star. As I gazed at the plethora of sparkling distant suns I searched for the star that was my soul.

MARTHA KRIPPKE

DESERT THOUGHTS

 THE DESERT is a place of insight. In its uncluttered
openness the mind becomes still and empty of
distracting chatter, creating space for the quiet spirit. As the Sufi
poet Omar Khayyam perceived, in the desert's eternal barrenness
we can feel ourselves to be as temporary as snow fallen on the
sand. Things appear differently in the desert. What value are all the
riches of the world, compared with a single drop of water to slake
a parched throat? Life and death stand out more plainly against the
clear desert horizon. Under the relentless gaze of the life-giving
and life-destroying sun, one is closer to death and more alive.

The worldly hopes men set their hearts upon

Turn ashes — or it prospers; and anon

Like snow upon the desert's dusty face

Lighting a little hour or two — is gone.

Think, in this batter'd Caravanserai

Whose doorways are alternate night and day,

How Sultan after Sultan with his pomp

Abode his hour or two, and went his way.

OMAR KHAYYAM

The sun gives life to
everything;
but in the desert it is the
angel of death.

TRADITIONAL BEDOUIN SAYING

I have driven across the Sahara five times now, and each time I touch death. You need to know what you are doing. One small fault with the truck and you're finished. But if you prepare properly and take precautions it is safer than you might think. Despite this, each year a number of people who try making the crossing will perish in the attempt. The most common reason is following mirages. If they just trusted the compass they would be fine, but seeing what they take to be habitation or an oasis they drive sometimes miles off course and that can be fatal. I have often mused about this as I've driven over that dusty expanse. It increasingly feels to me that if I could stop following mirages in my life I might get less lost in the turmoil of anxiety that has plagued me since I was a child. I guess that for some people the idea of crossing the Sahara is fearful and intimidating. For me it is inspiring and refreshing. When I cross the desert I've got a map and a compass – for the rest of my life I have neither and end up simply following mirages.

HUGH HOLGER

All sunshine makes a desert

ARAB PROVERB

It is the sandstorms that shape the stone statues of the desert.
It is the struggles of life that form a person's character.

NATIVE AMERICAN PROVERB

Fear Allah like a sandstorm.

BEDOUIN SAYING

In the desert water is worth more than gold.

ARAB PROVERB

Many desert stories are told to account for particular features of the landscape. One such is told of Sheik Hadji Abdul-Aziz, a Sufi dervish. He was traveling through a desert one summer in stifling sun. Parched and fatigued he spotted a beautiful green garden, full of fruit. He called to the gardener,

"My fellow man, in the name of Allah the merciful, give me a melon and I will give you my prayers." The gardener replied, "I'm not interested in your prayers, give me your money." The dervish answered, "But I am a beggar and have no money. I am sweating and thirsty, all I need is one of your melons." The gardener rebuffed him again saying, "Well go to the Nile and drink there." So the

dervish lifted his eyes to heaven and prayed,

"O Allah, You who quenched the thirst of Ismail
by creating the fountain of Zem-Zem in the midst
of the desert, will you allow one of your creatures
to die of thirst?"

Hardly had these words left his lips than a gentle
dew began to fall, refreshing his weary body.
After this miracle the gardener knew he was in
the presence of a holy man loved by Allah, and
he quickly offered him one of his melons. Hadji
Abdul-Aziz rebuffed him saying, "Keep it foolish
man. Your melons will become as hard as your
heart and this garden as barren as your soul."
Right away the melons turned to blocks of
stone and the land to sand – the very stones and
sand that can be seen at that spot to this day.

A greedy Caliph was very attached to his wealth, so the Sufi sage Shaqiq asked him, "Would you give one half of your kingdom to someone who could provide you with a drink of water if you were in the desert dying of thirst?" The Caliph said he would. Shaqiq then asked "Would you give the other half of your kingdom to someone able to help you pass that water if you had become unable to do so?" The Caliph again agreed that he would. "Why then do you value your kingdom so highly," asked Shaqiq, "when you would give it away in return for a drink of water which would itself not even stay with you?"

SUFI TEACHING STORY

WISDOM OF THE WILDERNESS

THE GOSPEL OF MATTHEW describes Jesus being led into the desert to be tested by the Devil. Going alone into the wilderness to find God and face your demons is an ancient spiritual tradition that is still practiced in shamanic cultures throughout the world. Native Americans, for example, practice the Vision Quest in which a quester will fast and pray alone in a remote and wild location for a number of days. During this time, he or she will receive visions and be spiritually tested. Being isolated in the desert is a lonely and life-threatening undertaking. The spiritual seeker who voluntarily undergoes such an ordeal is choosing to face his or her fear of death and solitude in a direct and powerfully transformative way.

Jesus was led by the spirit into the desert to be tempted by the Devil. After forty days and forty nights he was very hungry. The tempter appeared to him and said, "If you are the Son of God magically change these stones into loaves of bread." Jesus replied "The scripture teaches 'Man shall not live by bread alone, but by every word from the mouth of God.'"

Then the Devil took him to a holy city and placed him on a high pinnacle. "If you are the Son of God," he said, "then throw yourself off. For scripture says 'He will charge his angels with protecting you and they will bear you up in case you should dash your foot against a stone.'" Jesus replied "Yes that is true, but scripture also says 'You should not tempt the Lord your God.'"

After this the Devil took him to a high mountain from which could be seen the magnificence of all the kingdoms of the world. "I will give you all of this," he said "if you fall down and worship me." Jesus replied "Away with you Satan! Scripture says 'You shall worship the Lord your God and serve only Him.'"

Then the Devil left Jesus alone and angels came to him and took care of him.

THE GOSPEL OF MATTHEW

The Gnostics were early Christian heretics who inhabited the Egyptian deserts. Some of their lost gospels were discovered in 1945 hidden in a cave at Nag Hammadi in Upper Egypt. One text, called Zostrianos, relates how a spiritual master attained enlightenment. First he removed all physical desires and calmed the "chaos in the mind" with meditation. He then tells us, "After I had set myself straight, I had a vision of the perfect child." Following this experience of the divine presence he wandered out into the desert, half expecting to be killed by wild animals. Here he finally received a vision of "the Messenger of the Knowledge of the Eternal Light." He encourages us, "Why are you hesitating? Seek when you are sought. When you are invited, listen. Look at the Light. Do not be led astray to your destruction."

ZOSTRIANOS

*I*n the old days, when a man went out to get visions – to the wilderness, or a high place, a desert, somewhere all alone – well then, in the old days he didn't know if he would ever come back again. He found that place and made a circle in the sand, then he sat in the circle and waited for visions. Days and nights with no food and just a blanket – now after some time the vision comes. He smokes the sacred tobacco and prays and he is singing all his heart to the Great Spirit, saying "Give me a vision." He gets very scared out there. But his medicine protects him until the vision comes.

ROLLING THUNDER

*A man finds out who
he is in the wilderness.
His soul speaks to him.*

JAMES RUNNING DEER

When a Cleverman go to the outback, he not takin' a holiday you know. He healin' somethin' or someone. Healin' some person, like curin' sick person. So listen me story. I'm tellin'. Cleverman go out where nothin' livin'. But he livin'. He not laughin'. He gonna make rain or somethin'. He all alone but really he not there. He some place else. Dreamin' some place. He know what he doin' alright.

BILL BUNGABE

*T*he Sufis revere Jesus as a great prophet. They
know him as "Issa son of Miryam," and tell
teaching stories that reveal his wisdom. In the New
Testament when Jesus is tested by the Devil, he wisely
resists the temptation to use his magical powers. A Sufi
teaching story relates what happens to some of his
disciples who were not so wise.

Issa was walking in the desert near Jerusalem with his followers who begged him to tell them the secret Name by which he had the power to raise the dead. He said, "If I tell you, you won't use it wisely." They replied, "We are ready Master and it will strengthen our faith." "You don't know what you are asking," he told them. They insisted, however, so reluctantly he revealed to them the secret Name. A little later these people left Issa and came upon a heap of whitened bones. "Let's try out that magic Name," one of them suggested. Immediately they did so, the bones became clothed with flesh and were transformed into a wild beast that tore them all to shreds. Such is the danger of knowledge without the wisdom to use it.

SUFI TEACHING STORY

The Sufis believe that there is no universal right way to approach God, and that each seeker must follow the dictates of his or her own heart. This moral is brought out by the Sufi master Jalaludin Rumi in an amusing tale about another desert prophet, the Jewish leader Moses. In the Bible, Moses hears God speak to him from a burning bush while he is leading the Jewish people out of exile in Egypt across the desert to the Promised Land. At that time God reveals himself as a grand lawgiver who presents Moses with the Ten Commandments. In this Sufi story, however, God presents a friendly, compassionate face, and rebukes Moses for his spiritual grandiosity.

One day Moses came across a humble old shepherd in the desert, who was privately talking to God. The shepherd's tone was relaxed and familiar. He told God how he wanted to help Him: to pick the lice off of Him; to wash His clothes; to kiss His feet and hands. He ended his prayer with "When I think of You all I can say is Ahhhh!" Moses was appalled and exclaimed "Do you realize that you are talking to the Creator of Heaven and Earth, not to your old uncle?!" The shepherd felt very foolish and asked Moses if he thought God would ever forgive him. However, as the shepherd began to wander off sadly into the desert to repent, a divine voice spoke to Moses rebuking him.

"Moses, what to you seems wrong is right to him. One man's poison is another man's honey. Purity and impurity, sloth and diligence – what do these matter to me? I am above all that. Ways of worship can not be put in ranks as better or worse. It is all praise and it is all right. It is the worshiper who is glorified by worship – not I. I don't listen to the words. I look inside at the humility. Only that low and open emptiness is real. Forget language – I want burning, burning! Be friends with this fire. Burn up your grand ideas and special words!"

JALALUDIN RUMI

A man knocked on a door. "Who's there?" asked God.
"Me" replied the man. "Go away then," said God.
The man left and wandered in the arid desert until he
realized his error. He returned to the door and knocked
again. "Who's there?" asked God. "You," replied the man.
"Then come in," said God, "There's no room here for two."

SUFI TEACHING STORY

DESERT FATHERS

THE MOST FAMOUS of all desert mystics are the early Christian recluses who made their homes in solitary caves or small communities out in the wildernesses of the Middle East – earning themselves the name of the "Desert Fathers". Their title of "Abba" means simply "Father". One of their centers was called Cellia because of the number of cells scattered around the desert. This environment was utterly desolate and the cells were so separated that no one could see or hear his neighbor. In this huge quiet these mystics prayed, fasted, and received their visions. The Desert Fathers were called "anchorites" meaning "rule-breakers" because they had abandoned all their public duties. Their lives were hard and simple, yet from this crude existence came a capacity for kindness and wisdom.

Abba Zeno said, "If someone wants to be heard by God, then before he prays for his own soul, or for anything else, let him pray with all his heart for his enemies. If he does this God will hear everything he asks."

Amma Syncletica said "At first those who are going towards God experience great battles and much suffering, but afterwards ineffable joy. It is like lighting a fire. To begin with you get choked with smoke and end up crying. For, as it is written, 'Our God is a consuming fire.'"

Abba Lot said to Abba Joseph, "I fast, I pray, I meditate. As far as I can I purify my thoughts. What else can I do?" Abba Joseph stretched out his old hands toward heaven and his fingers became like lamps of light. He said, "If you will it, you can become all fire."

A brother was talking to Abba Matoes about the virtue of loving one's enemies. Abba Matoes replied, "As for myself, I have yet to manage truly to love those that love me."

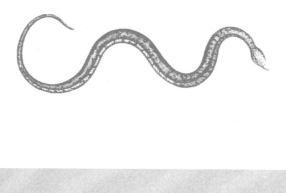

Blessed Anthony was praying one day when a voice said, "Anthony, you are still not of the stature of the tanner in the city." So Anthony went to find the tanner and said to him, "I have left the desert to find you. Please tell me about your good works." The tanner replied, "I am not aware of having done any good works. When I get up, before I start work, I affirm that the whole of this city, great and small, will go to the kingdom of God, while I alone will go to eternal punishment for the evil in my heart. That is all." Anthony said, "You work in the city with all its distractions while I sit in solitude in the desert, but I have not come near the wisdom of these words."

*A hermit who could cast out demons asked
them, "Is it fasting that gives me the power
to banish you?"
The demons replied, "We do not eat."
He asked, "Is it my long vigils?"
The demons replied, "We do not sleep."
He asked, "Is it retreat from the world?"
The demons replied, "We live in the deserts."
He asked, "What is it, then, that gives me
power over you?"
The demons replied, "Nothing can overcome us
but humility."*

AMMA THEODORA

A brother asked Abba Peomen, "How should I behave in my desert cell?" Abba Peomen replied, "Wherever you live, live like a stranger and do not expect your words to have any influence, then you will be at peace."